AFTER THE FIRE & THE PARTICULARS

ALSO BY MATTHEW MacKENZIE

Bears

AFTER THE FIRE & THE PARTICULARS

MATTHEW MacKENZIE

PLAYWRIGHTS CANADA PRESS
TORONTO

First edition: May 2023
Printed and bound in Canada by Rapido Books, Montreal

Jacket and author photos © Alexis McKeown

Playwrights Canada Press
202-269 Richmond St. W., Toronto, ON M5V 1X1
416.703.0013 | info@playwrightscanada.com | www.playwrightscanada.com

LIBRARY AND ARCHIVES CANADA CATALOGUING IN PUBLICATION
Title: After the fire : & The particulars / Matthew MacKenzie.
Other titles: Plays. Selections | Particulars
Names: MacKenzie, Matthew, author. | MacKenzie, Matthew. Particulars
Description: Two plays.
Identifiers: Canadiana (print) 20230167691 | Canadiana (ebook) 20230167721 | ISBN 9780369104090 (softcover) | ISBN 9780369104106 (EPUB) | ISBN 9780369104113 (PDF)
Classification: LCC PS8625.K454 A6 2023 | DDC C812/.6—dc23

Playwrights Canada Press operates on land which is the ancestral home of the Anishinaabe Nations (Ojibwe / Chippewa, Odawa, Potawatomi, Algonquin, Saulteaux, Nipissing, and Mississauga), the Wendat, and the members of the Haudenosaunee Confederacy (Mohawk, Oneida, Onondaga, Cayuga, Seneca, and Tuscarora), as well as Metis and Inuit peoples. It always was and always will be Indigenous land.

We acknowledge the financial support of the Canada Council for the Arts, the Ontario Arts Council (OAC), Ontario Creates, and the Government of Canada for our publishing activities.

Canada Council for the Arts | Conseil des arts du Canada
ONTARIO ARTS COUNCIL
CONSEIL DES ARTS DE L'ONTARIO
an Ontario government agency
un organisme du gouvernement de l'Ontario
Canada
ONTARIO CREATES | ONTARIO CRÉATIF

AFTER THE FIRE

FOREWORD

BY ELDER JO-ANN SADDLEBACK

Matthew MacKenzie and I have had many discussions about his many works over the years. He immersed himself on the journey of finding out who he is, what his culture is, what it means to his life, and how it influences what he writes and how he now interprets the world. He has become a significant philosopher and historian as he grounds himself in his Indigenous roots while keeping the best of what he learned about the rest of the world.

Matthew's *After the Fire* is a story about a small group of friends and relatives finding their lives after the fire that nearly destroyed and burned down most of Fort McMurray, Alberta. Matthew uses his accomplished skills like an impressionist artist paints a moment in life. He gives us people trying to find the ordinary, a supposedly familiar day of mundane tasks and mundane conversations, much as they were programmed to, in this slice-of-life piece. But nothing is the same and they are not doing the same things and their conversations are incredibly revealing. What was supposed to keep them grounded is now wholly unfamiliar. His characters seem aimless in trying to put together their lives, not realizing how the fire has impacted them and therefore changed them forever—changed their days, changed their conversations, and changed the things they do and of what they are capable.

Matthew's accomplishment is not just in the writing of the play, it is in all he gives us. He is a philosopher, a realist, a cultural interpreter, and a historian. He gives us a clear understanding of the human condition through the many transformations of his characters. Matthew shares his depth of understanding about Cree and Métis cultures, how Indigenous people can step into and out of the two worlds that surround them.

His characters are in a huge struggle to find their lives again, for things to be the same and to return to as they were before the fire. But nothing is the same—they are now living unconsciously in a life so much bigger than their own and all the rules have changed.

Matthew easily guides us through how these two worlds work together and how they collide. Only with a good working understanding of the cultures and life can a writer become an artist, and Matthew has accomplished this. He has my deep respect because of his talent in sharing Cree culture through his writing, as the good medicine it is. He is proven the best ambassador to bring the realities of these two worlds together so we all may get a glimpse of how they exist in the same space, on the same day, and in the same events. It has been one of the pleasures in my husband's and my life to know him, spend time with him, advise him, and have the best conversations. It is the spice of life and the best kind of magic humans are good at. It is what makes our stories.

As a prominent Indigenous playwright, Matthew takes his place as a Storyteller and experienced artist in the world.

Jo-Ann Saddleback is involved in many Indigenous arts initiatives, including advising artists and art groups. She is currently Elder-in-Residence for the Edmonton Public Library and supports, promotes, and helps to establish Indigenous writers, artists, filmmakers, and Knowledge Keepers.

A first iteration of *After the Fire* was produced under the title *Bust* by Theatre Network at the Roxy on Gateway, Edmonton, from February 7 to 26, 2017, with the following cast and creative team:

Barry: Christopher Schulz
Carmell: Louise Lambert
Laura: Lora Brovold
Ty: Brandon Coffey

Director: Bradley Moss
Set and Costume Designer: Cory Sincennes
Lighting Designer: Scott Peters
Composer/Sound Designer: Darrin Hagen
Stage Manager: Molly Pearson

The play was later produced by Punctuate! Theatre in collaboration with Dreamspeakers and Native Earth Performing Arts at The Theatre Centre, Toronto, in January 2019, with the following cast and creative team:

Barry: Sheldon Elter
Carmell: Louise Lambert
Laura: Kaitlyn Riordan
Ty: Jesse Gervais

Director: Brendan McMurtry-Howlett
Producer: Sheiny Satanove
Sound Designer: Dean Musani
Set, Costume, and Props Designer: Alison Yanota
Stage Manager: Natasha Bean-Smith
Lighting Designer: Kaileigh Krysztofiak

CHARACTERS

Laura: Midthirties, works at the animal shelter.
Carmell: Midthirties, hair salon owner/operator.
Barry: Midthirties, Métis, underemployed safety inspector.
Ty: Midthirties, Métis, unemployed heavy hauler operator.

SETTING

In and around Fort McMurray, late summer, after the fire.

Cosmic overture.

Sounds of industry. Sounds of hockey. Sounds of Ducks quacking.

LAURA, CARMELL, TY, and BARRY stand in silhouette.

LAURA: Will the insurance come through?

CARMELL: You gotta keep your head on a swivel.

LAURA: When he goes to the garage, what does he do?

CARMELL: The salon will not foreclose.

TY: You've got your guilt, you've got your self-loathing, you've got your booze.

CARMELL: No one is going to bail you out but you.

BARRY: A banditry of Chickadees . . .

TY: Keep your head up!

BARRY: Will fly together for life—

CARMELL: That's it, hon!

A post is hit. A heavy hauler dumps its load. Ducks land on water. The four clap in unison once.

LAURA: Ethanol, benzene, bitumen . . .

BARRY: Mallards, Buffleheads, Scaups . . .

LAURA: Dip and rinse.

TY: Benzoylmethylecgonine.

CARMELL: Say it again.

TY: Benzoylmethylecgonine.

CARMELL: Sounds like a good time.

BARRY: Grey Jay, Blue Jay, Mourning Warbler.

LAURA: Dip and rinse.

BARRY: Half-dozen goslings. Snow Geese, I think.

TY: This is what I look at every morning in the mirror.

LAURA: Dip and rinse.

CARMELL: There is more out there than just driving a heavy hauler.

TY: I am Alberta, motherfucker.

A bench door is slammed. High-pressure steam is released. A Duck struggles in toxic tailings. The four clap in unison twice.

BARRY: She sees it coming.

CARMELL: It's just a game.

BARRY: The world aflame.

TY: Sounds like heartburn to me.

BARRY: I pretended not to see.

LAURA: You gotta be gentle with yourself.

CARMELL: A stupid game.

LAURA: Like you are with me.

BARRY: The whole city pretended not to see.

TY: Duck and weave.

CARMELL: But it means everything.

LAURA: Dip and rinse.

BARRY: Is it too late?

A fire erupts as the four clap in unison three times. Lights to half.

CARMELL: C'mon, ladies, show them what you're made of.

LAURA: That's it, that's it.

TY: Keep your head up.

CARMELL: Easy outlet.

LAURA: Tape to tape.

CARMELL: Don't give her space like that.

LAURA: C'mon, ref.

TY: That's it—that's it!

CARMELL: There you go.

TY: Come on, ref!

LAURA: Stay hydrated.

CARMELL: You need to stay between the attacker and the net.

LAURA: Offside.

CARMELL: You've gotta be kidding.

LAURA: That was offside.

TY: End to end.

LAURA: You can do this.

CARMELL: Collapse to the net!

LAURA: You just have to focus.

Lights fade like dying embers. The four again stand in silhouette.

BARRY: A Chickadee's "dee-dees" are an alarm. The closer a threat gets, the more "dee-dees" a Chickadee will sound.

(in Cree) Is it too late?

LAURA and CARMELL stand at the edge of the forest with Timbits and Double Doubles. LAURA clutches her purse close. Silence.

LAURA: They didn't give us any chocolate.

Pause.

That means someone came in and took only chocolate.

Pause.

They shouldn't allow that.

Long pause.

CARMELL: There's no rule that you have to get an assortment.

Pause.

LAURA: It just seems implicit.

Long pause.

They wouldn't allow that in Saudi Arabia. They've got an honour code.

Pause.

CARMELL: That extends to doughnuts.

Pause.

LAURA: Yes.

Pause.

CARMELL: You've heard this, or you know this?

Pause.

LAURA: Both.

Long pause.

CARMELL: So you know you'd have to cover up if you were going for doughnuts.

LAURA: Yes.

CARMELL: And that your husband would have to escort you to the doughnut shop.

LAURA: Barry likes doughnuts.

CARMELL: And that he would have to ask for an assortment because you wouldn't be allowed to talk to the staff.

LAURA: Not the end of the world.

CARMELL: And that you would have to walk behind him before and after he has made your purchase, out of deference.

Beat.

LAURA: That's ridiculous.

CARMELL: What's ridiculous is considering trading your basic rights and freedoms for doughnuts.

Pause.

LAURA: Just relax.

CARMELL: I'm relaxed.

Pause.

LAURA: I'm not saying we're going.

CARMELL: You are actively entertaining the possibility.

LAURA: We are not moving.

CARMELL: No, you'd be running away.

LAURA: Nobody's running away.

CARMELL: That's right. So you just relax, okay?

Silence.

LAURA: I . . .

Pause.

I . . .

Pause.

I . . .

CARMELL: You don't have to say anything.

Pause.

LAURA: Okay.

Cosmic dissonance. LAURA *stares up at the moon.*

The moon shines bright on Fort McMurray . . . the city that never stops working. Like a hockey game that keeps going and going.

Pause.

When you're coaching, what are you thinking?

Short pause.

CARMELL: What do you mean?

Short pause.

LAURA: Like when you're speaking, and the girls are all listening.

Pause.

CARMELL: I'm thinking I want to beat the other team.

Pause. LAURA *shakes her head.*

LAURA: I wouldn't know what to say.

Pause.

Ultimately, I'm thinking the same thing. But I wouldn't know what to say.

Pause.

CARMELL: You coordinate dozens of volunteers and several employees.

LAURA: That's not the same thing.

Short pause.

That's in the event of an emergency.

Pause.

CARMELL: Saving the lives of animals is more important than hockey.

Short pause.

LAURA: But I'm responding.

Beat.

I don't lead an attack to eliminate the threat to those pets pre-emptively.

Pause.

CARMELL: There are different ways to lead.

Pause.

LAURA: What good are you doing, coordinating dozens of volunteers and several employees, when the world is burning and you tell them to leave?

Pause.

CARMELL: You had them take all the animals from the shelter and evacuate. That's taking the lead.

Pause.

LAURA: Hundreds of pets died.

CARMELL: You are not responsible for what happened to those other animals.

LAURA: Then who is?

CARMELL: No one is. The fire is.

LAURA: But everyone got out. Eighty thousand of us.

CARMELL: Yes. It was miraculous.

LAURA: Not for those pets . . .

Pause.

CARMELL: Calm, cool, and collected, that's all that's expected.

LAURA: I don't think Nan was talking about situations like this.

CARMELL: It's a mantra. It extends to all situations.

Pause.

LAURA: Haley and Taryn are with Nan now.

CARMELL nods.

CARMELL: Mom and Dad took them over with Declan to watch *Spaceballs*.

Pause.

LAURA: And we . . .

CARMELL: We went to the game. We grabbed coffees. Then we went to BP's.

Pause. LAURA shakes her head.

LAURA: I need to call Barry.

CARMELL: We're in the middle of nowhere, there's no reception.

LAURA goes to open her purse.

No—

LAURA drops the purse—it lands with a thud. LAURA backs away from it.

LAURA: Oh sweet Christ—oh sweet Christ—

CARMELL: Breathe.

LAURA slowly pops a squat, trying to control her breathing.

LAURA: Should Declan be watching *Spaceballs*? He's only six.

CARMELL: Yes. It's over his head.

LAURA: Haley reaggravated her groin injury. I should be with her, helping her stretch.

CARMELL: After we've finished this.

LAURA: It took her so long to recover the last time . . .

CARMELL: She's eleven, she'll heal fine.

LAURA: But hockey, hockey's the only thing that makes her happy since we lost everything . . .

CARMELL: We need to focus.

CARMELL picks up the purse.

We need to focus on getting rid of this purse and then getting to Boston Pizza.

CARMELL pulls LAURA to her feet.

Fishbowl Fridays.

A whistle sounds in the distance.

Shift change. Let's go.

CARMELL takes LAURA by the wrist, pulling her off. Lights rise to reveal a scene of devastation where the fire blew through. Jack Pine stand like burnt matchsticks. TY enters with a Diet Pepsi. He stands and stares. BARRY enters with a spade.

They survey the area.

BARRY: How deep?

TY: Seven. Eight feet. Deep.

Pause. BARRY picks a spot and starts to dig. TY walks around the area.

Think I'm allergic to aspartame. Feels like I'm walkin' in a dream.

BARRY digs.

I love the smell of a summer night . . .

TY inhales deep. BARRY digs.

Would come out here before the fire . . . Peaceful.

TY walks.

Quadin' around with Declan and Taryn, scarin' up Grouse . . . That Declan, he's fearless. Reminds me of myself.

BARRY digs. TY kicks at something.

They say the fire's still burnin'. Beneath the ground. They say it could stay burnin' . . . for years.

Cosmic dissonance. TY pops a seed.

That was somethin' . . . Cheerin' on Haley and Taryn. Timbits, Novice, Atom . . . Taryn shootin' the puck 'n' Haley stoppin' 'em.

TY spits.

Who'd'a thought they'd be playin' together in the provincial championships, our daughters.

BARRY digs.

We never played in any championships. Not even close. The Chiefs got their asses kicked all over the province . . .

BARRY digs. TY pops a seed.

Carmell . . . she's got passion. That's what makes her such a good coach. She has to win. Doesn't matter what game. She plays canasta like it's a blood sport. She's like a wolf, constantly on the hunt.

TY spits.

Laura and Carmell, they make a good pair. Sisters, sure, but Laura's more than just a trainer. She's like one of those flag bearers in a cavalry charge—everyone goin' down around her, but she's still waving the team's colours in the air.

TY pops a seed.

That's what any elite team needs: a wolf behind the bench and a die hard leading the charge into battle.

The call of a Nighthawk.

Touching ceremony before the game. How they marched out all our first responders, like they were soldiers back from war.

They shoulda had Laura up there.

TY *pops a seed.*

People care a lot more about their animals than they do about each other. Laura runnin' from house to house, freeing people's cats and dogs so that they wouldn't be consumed by the fire . . .

BARRY *swats at a Mosquito.* TY *spits.*

They'd probably be making a bigger deal about it if it hadn't technically been illegal, ignoring the mandatory evacuation order . . . But whoever heard of a hero following all the rules?

BARRY *digs.* TY *shakes his head.*

They say they don't know how the fire got started. Maybe a campfire. Maybe one of those exploding smart phones. Maybe an all-terrain vehicle.

Don't know how they go about investigating something like that . . .

BARRY *swats at a Mosquito.*

Even if they do figure out who started it, I don't see how that'd change much.

TY *swats at a Mosquito.*

I mean, let's say it was some teenager's cigarette. Are we gonna string him up? Everyone's smoked somethin' at some point in their lives, so it could've been any one of us. Unless they determine someone intentionally started a fire with a cigarette and then fed it kindling and fanned the flames and shit.

BARRY digs.

"We live in a time of blame" is what my therapist likes to say. Nobody is interested in truth anymore. We just want someone to point a finger at.

BARRY digs.

Maybe that's why I like to party. Self-sabotage. Eh, Barry? I'm like a New Age martyr or something.

BARRY digs.

Got no one to blame? Blame Ty.

LAURA emerges in half light.

LAURA: Even though we've lost everything, compared to a lot of people, Barry and I are doing okay. It's important to count your blessings. With me and Barry . . . it's like we're falling in love all over again.

Full light. LAURA and CARMELL move through dense Boreal cover.

How do you maintain your stamina, in the face of it all?

They move.

CARMELL: My house didn't burn down.

LAURA: No, I know . . .

They move.

But with Ty losing his job, and the divorce . . .

CARMELL: Hot yoga.

LAURA: Huh?

CARMELL: I just crank the space heater and fuckin' give 'er.

LAURA: Never got into yoga . . .

CARMELL: Happy people don't.

They move.

LAURA: But you're happy, with Greenpeace?

CARMELL: He has a name.

LAURA: Sorry.

CARMELL: I'm happy with Greenpeace, that's right.

They frighten up an animal in the bush.

LAURA: Where is he now?

CARMELL: Kuala Lumpur.

LAURA: He sure gets around.

CARMELL: Yep.

LAURA: Slaggin' us all over the globe.

CARMELL: He doesn't pass judgment. He just goes around trying to raise awareness about the effects of climate change and hoping that no one torches his hybrid again.

They move.

LAURA: Greenpeace should've been there tonight.

CARMELL: Greenpeace doesn't care about hockey. It's refreshing.

LAURA: He seems totally oblivious to the fact that his Petiole affects Declan's breathing.

CARMELL: What do you mean?

LAURA: Whenever Greenpeace comes in the room, Declan starts wheezing.

CARMELL: He's a sensitive little guy.

LAURA: Like Ty.

LAURA and CARMELL exit. TY hits a Mosquito on BARRY's back.

TY: Got 'im. Big sucker.

TY flicks the Mosquito off his palm, chuckling.

First the fire, then the flood, now Mosquitos at plague levels . . . Endofdays . . . Endofdays, Bear.

TY pops a seed.

If you'd'a told me five years ago in Puerto Vallarta that this is where we'd be now, I'd'a laughed at you.

BARRY *digs.* TY *shakes his head, walking around.*

We should go on another all-inclusive. When things pick back up again.

BARRY *digs.*

The two families.

BARRY *digs.*

Eh, Bear?

BARRY *digs.*

Diggin' for seashells.

BARRY *digs.*

Eatin' tortillas.

BARRY *digs.*

Wackin' pinatas.

BARRY *digs.*

Drikin' pina coladas.

BARRY *digs.*

Fuckin' kitesailin'.

BARRY *digs.*

Got somethin' against Mexico now?

BARRY: Huh?

TY: Because you were the one who pushed to go to Vallarta.

BARRY: I don't know what you're talkin' about.

TY: Jesus, I said we should go for another all-inclusive, when things pick back up.

BARRY: Yeah.

BARRY digs.

TY: Does the body good, to escape winter for a bit.

BARRY digs.

Take the kids to a bull fight.

BARRY: Mm.

TY: You know I wouldn't take the kids to a bull fight—Laura'd have a fit.

BARRY: No, I know.

TY: You haven't listened to a thing I've said.

BARRY: I have.

TY: Bullshit.

BARRY digs.

BARRY: I've got a lot on my mind.

TY: Welcome to the club.

BARRY: We came here to dig.

BARRY digs.

TY: So you wanna dig in complete silence?

BARRY stops digging.

BARRY: You're not freakin' out?

TY: Of course I'm freakin' out.

BARRY: You don't seem like you're freakin' out.

TY: It's called a game face.

BARRY: You seem like you're enjoying yourself.

TY: People experience emotions in different ways.

BARRY shakes his head. He starts digging again.

BARRY: I'm worried. About Laura.

BARRY digs.

TY: Well . . . That's understandable.

BARRY: What if they run into trouble?

TY: You don't have to worry. She's with Carmell.

BARRY: Laura panics around authority. She can barely make it through airport security.

TY: Laura's never done a bad thing in her life.

BARRY: That's the problem, Ty.

TY: Carmy can talk her way out of anything—I've never met anyone calmer in a crisis, believe me.

TY pops a seed.

I'm tryin' to focus on somethin' positive here. I'm talkin' about bringin' our families together.

TY spits.

After this all blows over.

A tsunami of fire. LAURA and CARMELL move through thick Boreal cover.

LAURA: It's gotta be tough, having us underfoot.

CARMELL: Me and the kids love having you guys around.

LAURA: We appreciate it, we really do. I mean, Haley and Taryn already spent almost every waking moment together anyway.

They move.

A real role reversal . . . My little sister, helping me out.

CARMELL: We're happy to.

They move.

LAURA: It's weird not having Ty around. It feels like we kicked him out, even though, you know, we didn't. I keep expecting to see him flipping burgers out at the barbecue or chuckin' the kids around on the trampoline.

CARMELL: He hasn't died. You can see him whenever you like.

LAURA: Oh, I know. He just reminds me of one of our rescues at the shelter, you know? Thinking of him in your guys' RV makes my heart ache a little, is all.

CARMELL: Ty's not some abandoned animal.

LAURA: I know.

CARMELL: Do you? Because to hear you talk about him, you'd think Tyson shit gold.

LAURA: He has his faults, but then so have you.

They move. TY *in half light.*

TY: I'm talkin' grit. I'm talkin' hustle—it doesn't matter what the other team's got on you. So long as you've got heart, you'll get the "w." Provided you aren't competing against any extraneous factors . . .

Full light.

For the girls to work that hard. For them to battle back like that . . . For them to play that well and then lose it all because of something they couldn't control . . . That's heartbreak. That's the sort of thing that's gonna turn our girls sour on the game. Sour on life.

But what's done is done.

A cosmic shiver.

Now we just gotta keep things simple.

A cosmic shudder. Pause. LAURA *and* CARMELL *exit.* TY *pops a seed.*

Tried to keep things simple after we were forced to leave town. That's why we sent Taryn up to that Camp Maskepetoon.

TY spits.

They get them doin' all sorts of stuff—canoein', campin', beanbag tossin' . . .

TY pops a seed.

This one kid, he's really gettin' on Taryn's nerves. Talkin' about how Chief Maskepetoon scalped his wife alive, and that his ghost was gonna scalp the girls in the night. Pretty kooky. He didn't know Taryn's part Cree.

TY spits, pops another seed.

So they're all sittin' around the campfire, singin' songs and roastin' marshmallows—when this same kid that's been buggin' Taryn starts singin', "The bush, the bush, the bush is on fire. We don't need no water, let the motherfucker burn, burn Fort McMurray, burn."

BARRY: Aw.

TY spits.

TY: Ya.

BARRY: Taryn.

TY: She's a sensitive one.

TY pops another.

And she's obviously feelin' a lot of emotions, what with her parents separatin' and her cousin's house burnin' down and the racism . . . So she stands up, jerseys this little fucker, and starts wailin' on him.

BARRY: Good for Taryn.

TY: That's what I said!

TY spits.

But you know what those camp fucks did? They sent Taryn home.

BARRY: Oh, come on.

TY: Yeah.

TY pops another.

We didn't tell anyone . . .

He spits, pops another.

Don't want Taryn known as a loose cannon.

TY shakes his head.

But I've told her—I've always said, "Anyone says somethin' derogatory about you bein' Métis, you make 'em pay."

TY spits.

Heart of gold and a hell of a wrist shot . . . God I love that kid.

TY shakes his head. He pops a seed. BARRY digs.

You have been acting distant lately. Before tonight even. Like on another planet or something.

BARRY: Yeah . . . I dunno.

TY takes the spade from BARRY. He digs.

TY: We've hardly spoken since the evacuation order got lifted and we got let back into town.

BARRY: Yeah . . . I guess.

TY: I mean, your house burned down. I get it.

BARRY: Yeah. I dunno . . .

TY digs.

TY: Where's your mind been?

TY digs.

BARRY: My mind's been . . .

TY digs.

Wandering.

TY digs.

TY: Makes sense. Major disaster. Part-time hours. More time to think.

TY bangs soil off the spade.

Ever since I got laid off, I've been goin' fuckin' crazy.

BARRY: Yeah.

TY digs.

TY: Where do you "wander"?

BARRY: Huh?

TY: Where has your mind been "wandering" to?

BARRY: Oh, I dunno . . . All over.

TY digs.

I've been thinking a lot about plants and animals.

TY: Huh.

BARRY: When I'm driving. When I'm working. When I'm sleeping . . . Well, trying.

TY nods.

TY: Insomnia. Yuh. Haven't had a good night's sleep in months—but I still wake up at four-thirty every goddamn morning.

BARRY shakes his head.

BARRY: Not the kind of thinking that leaves you tossing and turning.

TY: You just lie there. Awake.

BARRY: No, I close my eyes. I'm in, like . . . a semi-conscious state.

Distant cosmic dissonance.

TY: Well . . . What do you see? When you close your eyes?

TY stops digging.

BARRY: Black-Capped Chickadees.

Pause. TY *starts digging again.*

TY: You better not be goin' Greenpeace on me.

BARRY *shakes his head.*

BARRY: Thinking about Black-Capped Chickadees doesn't mean I wanna take anybody's job away.

TY: Well sometimes you can't have it both ways.

BARRY: Like having Chickadees and prosperity.

TY: Got nothin' against Chickadees, just saying.

BARRY: You aren't saying anything.

TY: It's a figure of speech.

BARRY: That means nothing.

TY: Okay, I love Chickadees—I'll get fuckin' T-shirts made.

BARRY: You can't have a problem with every living thing just because Carmell is dating Greenpeace, Ty.

TY *stops digging.*

I'm sorry.

TY *waves him away.*

TY: No, it's okay.

Pause. TY *resumes digging.*

Just surprised me. Thought we were talkin' about Chickadees . . . not fuckin' heartbreak.

BARRY: I know you don't hate living things.

TY: Greenpeace doesn't have a monopoly on liking birds and trees. I commune with nature regularly.

BARRY: It's the northern way.

TY: The RV and water skis weren't designed for urban settings.

BARRY: Damn right.

TY: Even if I am living in my RV in an urban setting.

BARRY: Only temporarily.

TY leans on the spade.

TY: Fuck'sake.

LAURA and CARMELL wade through Muskeg.

LAURA: What's that like?

They wade.

Having children with someone but not being with them?

CARMELL: It's amazing.

LAURA: No, seriously.

CARMELL: Fuck, Laura, what do you want me to say? The kids love Ty. They look at me like I've banished the world's best dad to the RV.

LAURA: He is a devoted father.

They wade.

You're not gonna wanna hear this . . .

They wade.

. . . but I've gotta be honest. I'm still rootin' for Tyson. Seeing him at the games, how he lives and breathes every second Taryn's on the ice, how he puts Declan up on his shoulders so he can see plays developing—how he never questions your coaching—

CARMELL: Fucking please . . .

LAURA: No one knows what goes on between two people behind closed doors, but I think I know Ty pretty well. I've known him longer than you, and he's been my brother-in-law for fifteen years.

CARMELL: Fourteen.

LAURA: And he still is, as far as I'm concerned.

CARMELL pulls herself out of the Muskeg.

CARMELL: I think working at the shelter has messed with you. People aren't animals.

CARMELL exits.

LAURA: I'm sorry I'm upsetting you, but sometimes you need to tell people what they don't want to hear.

LAURA pulls herself out of the Muskeg and exits.

TY: You wanna hear somethin' insane?

TY waits to make sure BARRY is listening.

I actually miss waitin' an hour every morning at the drive-through.

BARRY: You grow accustomed to doing the same thing.

TY: No kidding.

BARRY: We're like Grizzlies—we thrive on routine.

TY: That's right—top of the food chain. We take what we like—Deer, Bighorn Sheep—

BARRY: Dandelions—

TY: We eat; we hold territory; we mate.

Pause. TY looks to the sky.

Oh Christ . . .

BARRY stops digging.

No. No. I'm okay.

Pause. BARRY starts digging again.

I mean, how do you work for twenty years at something, make real money, more money than your parents ever could'a dreamed, and you wake up one morning and you have nothing. Nothing.

BARRY: You don't have nothing.

TY: No, Barry. I've got credit-card payments; I've got truck payments; I've got RV payments; I've got quad payments; I've got house payments; I've got horse payments . . .

BARRY: Horse payments?

TY: I don't wanna talk about the horse.

TY walks it off.

I mean, I'm making house payments for a house I don't even live in.

BARRY: You're providing for your children.

TY: And Carm.

BARRY: And Carm.

TY: And her fuckin' boyfriend.

BARRY: He's not live-in.

TY shakes his head.

TY: I was workin' on my truck, 'cause somehow the hitch got fucked, and Carm drives up to serve me with papers. And all I can do is just lie there. Because she thinks I'm a loser. I think I'm a loser . . . She just stands there starin' at me, not sayin' a thing, and I just lie there . . . gettin' teabagged by my own truck nuts. And after fifteen years of being married, you wanna know the only thing she has say to me?

CARMELL emerges in light.

CARMELL: When're you gonna get rid of those things, Ty?

CARMELL disappears from the light.

TY: I mean, when did truck nuts become a bad thing?

BARRY: Everything has its time.

CARMELL and LAURA move through thick Muskeg.

LAURA: How did you know you weren't in love with Ty anymore?

CARMELL: I never fell out of love with Tyson.

LAURA: Then why . . . ?

CARMELL: Cocaine.

LAURA stops.

LAURA: Ty does cocaine?

CARMELL: Does Guadeloupé bleed from the eyes?

CARMELL exits. TY shakes his head, popping a seed. LAURA exits.

TY: Everything has it's time . . .

TY pops a seed.

You think Carmell's gonna marry Greenpeace?

BARRY stops digging briefly, wiping sweat from his face.

BARRY: Dunno.

TY spits. Shakes his head.

TY: Was sittin' in my truck with Taryn, waiting for Declan to get out of his singin' lesson, and Taryn turns to me and says, "Dad, we really shouldn't be idling."

TY and BARRY whistle simultaneously.

It made the hair on the back of my neck stand on end to hear Greenpeace's words comin' out of the mouth of my Taryn.

TY shakes his head. He pops a seed.

How often does he come around?

BARRY: Depends. He travels a lot.

TY: Fightin' the good fight . . .

TY spits, lobbing the seed.

How often would you say he comes by in a week, when he is in town?

BARRY: I don't keep tabs.

TY: Two? Three . . . ? Approximately?

BARRY: You should be focusing on yourself, Ty.

TY: What's that supposed to mean?

BARRY: It means I don't feel comfortable saying.

TY: Fine.

TY pops a seed.

BARRY: Carmell takin' us in has been huge, Tyson. I'm not gonna report on someone who's brought my family into their home.

The call of a Great Horned Owl briefly distracts BARRY.

TY: Yeah, I said "fine." I just don't see how that gives you the right to start with a counselling session.

BARRY: Forget I said anything.

TY *nods. He spits.*

TY: I mean, I respect you not sayin' anythin'. Respectin' Carmell's privacy.

TY *pops a seed.*

Just don't start waggin' your finger at me—'cause I wasn't sittin' on Queen Street sippin' a fuckin' latte when Fort McMurray was burning.

CARMELL *enters, pursued by* LAURA.

LAURA: I can't believe I'm hearing this for the first time.

CARMELL: Doesn't do anybody any good to air their dirty laundry.

LAURA: I'm your sister.

CARMELL: I realize.

LAURA: I thought you were the problem.

CARMELL: I realize.

CARMELL *and* LAURA *exit.* BARRY *suddenly stops digging.*

TY: What?

BARRY: Longhorned Whitespotted Beetle.

BARRY carefully scoops up the Beetle and relocates it.

TY: . . . What's so special . . . ?

BARRY: The Longhorned Whitespotted Beetle is critical to the Boreal Forest's rejuvenation after a fire. They chew burnt wood and transform it into soil. They're like nature's first responders.

TY: Huh.

BARRY: They congregate in unusually high numbers up here; they're attracted to all the fire from industry. Now they can finally be what they were meant to be.

TY stares at the Beetle.

TY: They're pretty fuckin' creepy, if you ask me.

BARRY looks out over the Forest floor.

BARRY: I have become obsessed with the flora and fauna of this place.

TY stares at BARRY.

TY: . . . Laura's always been big on animals. Makes sense that would rub off.

BARRY: It's more than an interest. It's like a burning fire has been kindled in my chest.

BARRY stands, picking up the spade again.

TY: Well . . .

BARRY goes back to digging.

How does this burning "manifest" itself?

BARRY digs.

BARRY: I've been keeping a record. Of birds and small animals. That I've found.

TY: Found.

BARRY: Around the ponds.

Short pause.

TY: Around the tailings ponds?

BARRY nods.

BARRY: I bring them home.

TY stares at BARRY.

TY: Jesus, Barry. That's like collecting toxic waste.

BARRY: I clean them, then freeze them. I keep them in zip-lock bags. In the deep freeze.

Short pause.

TY: In my deep freeze?

BARRY nods. He digs.

Does Carmy know? What you've been . . . collecting?

BARRY shakes his head.

BARRY: Never even noticed them, before the fire. I mean, sure, if a flock flew in . . . But a lot of birds and small animals go about their business solo, or in pairs.

TY: Sure.

BARRY: It's like the fire blowin' through here has allowed me to see things. Like, actually see things.

BARRY digs.

TY: What kinds of things?

BARRY: Vole. Pine Marten. Baby Beaver.

BARRY digs.

Night Heron. Mourning Warbler. Yellow-Bellied Flycatcher.

BARRY digs.

Half dozen Goslings. Couple of Sandpipers. Kingfisher.

BARRY digs.

Couple of Mallards. Bufflehead. Scaup. Three immature Grebes, I think.

BARRY digs.

Grey Jay. Blue Jay.

BARRY digs.

Two-headed Chickadee.

Silence. TY stares at BARRY. BARRY stops digging.

What I can't get out of my mind, when I lie in bed at night, are those Chickadees' eyes.

BARRY looks to the sky. Pause.

TY: Okay, well, that definitely sounds like insomnia to me.

BARRY: No . . . The Chickadee doesn't haunt me. It's like, through its eyes . . .

BARRY makes a sweeping motion with his arm.

I can see.

Pause. BARRY continues digging. CARMELL goes.

TY: Well . . . What do you see?

LAURA follows.

Through the Chickadees' eyes?

BARRY: I see rivers. I see lakes. I see Muskeg. I see Moose wading, Eagles soaring, Bison grazing, Whooping Crane dancing . . .

Then I see smoke rising. I see the Muskeg drained, the Woods chopped down, the Earth clawed away. I see the mines, like open wounds, beneath me.

Then I see the lakes of toxic tailings . . .

Pause. BARRY *stops digging.*

Finding that two-headed Chickadee . . . I think it was a sign.

TY: A sign.

BARRY: To stop walking around with my head in the sand.

Beat.

TY: Like the oil sands.

BARRY *shakes his head, digs.*

BARRY: It's not what I'm sticking my head in that's the thing—it's that I've been wilfully obstructing my vision.

CARMELL *and* LAURA *enter.*

LAURA: You've had no one to confide in, no one to lean on.

CARMELL: I speak to Barry.

LAURA *stops.*

LAURA: You told Barry and you didn't tell me?

CARMELL: He talks to Ty.

LAURA: You told Barry and he didn't tell me.

CARMELL: I asked him not to.

LAURA: Why would you tell Barry and not tell me?

CARMELL: I just thought you not knowing would be the best thing.

Beat.

LAURA: How do you mean?

CARMELL: I felt you knowing would complicate things.

CARMELL exits.

TY: Wilfully obstructing your vision . . .

LAURA exits.

Like looking at the love of your life kiss her new boyfriend but seeing nothing, even though you're looking right at them?

BARRY: Something along those lines.

TY: Except the love of your life is . . . the Muskeg.

BARRY: The two things aren't really the same.

TY: I'm just rolling with what you're saying.

BARRY: No, you're comparing your failed marriage with the state of the planet.

TY: Nothing's failed. I haven't thrown in the towel yet.

BARRY: I don't think it works like that.

TY: Once the economy picks back up, things will sort themselves out.

BARRY: Has it ever occurred to you that some of your problems can't be blamed on the price of crude, Ty?

TY: What's that supposed to mean?

BARRY: To hear you talk about it, you'd think you'd personally borne the brunt of the downturn.

TY: You're comin' on a bit strong.

BARRY: Being a grown-up isn't hard, Tyson.

TY: Oh, now I'm not a man.

BARRY: Sure you are. You're a man-child.

CARMELL and LAURA enter. TY takes the spade from BARRY and starts digging aggressively.

LAURA: Are you saying I'm judgmental?

CARMELL: No. I'm saying that you take everybody's perceived problems on as your own.

LAURA: No I don't.

CARMELL: Ha!

LAURA: Give me an example.

CARMELL: Rearranging my Tupperware.

LAURA: Ordering.

CARMELL: Making comments that my carpets haven't been cleaned in a while and then getting them cleaned yourself.

LAURA: That was a surprise!

CARMELL: It certainly was.

LAURA: I wanted to show you gratitude, for opening your home. And the comments were about the dust buildup—your son is an asthmatic.

CARMELL: That was fucked up.

CARMELL pulls ahead.

LAURA: Devoting yourself to the well-being of others isn't a bad thing.

CARMELL: No, it's your cross, Laura, and you carry it happily, like some pill-poppin' fifties housewife. I've gotta march through the bush with you out here and listen to how the fire is the best thing that's happened to your marriage since Barry figured out how to give proper head.

CARMELL exits.

TY: Last time I checked, I'm the one who had the wherewithal to drive out here.

LAURA exits.

BARRY: In a truck that could get repoed at any second.

TY: I'm figuring things out.

BARRY: It's a miracle Carmell still lets you see Declan and Taryn.

TY: She's loyal—and leave my kids out of this.

BARRY: You're goddamn right she's loyal. She somehow hasn't completely given up on you—but I gotta hear you piss and moan about how it's all so unfair.

TY: The cards are stacked against me, but I am taking responsibility for my life.

BARRY: Your idea of taking responsibility is pretty amazing, Ty.

CARMELL enters, pursued by LAURA.

TY: You been this hard on Laura since she's been out of work with the shelter burned down?

BARRY: Laura hasn't self-sabotaged, Tyson.

TY: Are you fuckin' listenin' to yourself, Barry? Laura's the fuckin' reason we're out here!

A cosmic shiver.

BARRY: Even now you won't admit to your own horseshit.

CARMELL and LAURA exit.

TY: You know what, you're right. I'm just a loser. A huge fuckin' loser.

BARRY: You're not a loser—you're just the type of person who if you give an inch, you'll take a mile. That's why I told Carmell she had to leave you.

TY stops digging.

TY: You told Carmy to leave me.

BARRY: I told her you won't change unless you're forced to.

Pause. TY starts digging again.

TY: Helluva guy—hell of a fuckin' guy.

CARMELL and LAURA enter.

LAURA: I have never called it "head."

CARMELL: No, you call it "going down there" like Barry's some priest and you're some developmentally delayed nun.

LAURA: Who cares how I describe it—it's how it feels that matters.

CARMELL: I've heard you two in the basement.

LAURA: You're listening to us?!

CARMELL: That's not an orgasm, Laura.

LAURA: That is private.

CARMELL: I've had more electric bowel movements.

TY searches the Forest floor for Beetles.

LAURA: Don't attack my marriage just because yours is failing.

CARMELL: It's failed—ya got me.

LAURA exits, CARMELL pursuing.

BARRY: What would you have done, Ty?

TY: I'd've stood by my friend, Barry.

BARRY: On coke you're not my friend.

LAURA follows.

TY: What's that supposed to mean?

BARRY: You're someone else entirely.

TY: Oh, now you and Carmy have really been talking.

BARRY: You're right, Ty. It's all just one big conspiracy to rob you of a good time.

TY: Well it's worked out pretty good for you and your family, with Uncle Ty livin' in his RV.

BARRY: You refusing to address your cocaine problem has provided the perfect opportunity for me, my wife, and my daughter to move into your home after ours burned down—you're right, Tyson.

TY: Yeah, and my deep freeze can hold just about every toxic abomination you can lay your hands on.

TY bangs a clump of dirt off the spade.

Once you've got a proper collection, you and Greenpeace can hold a press conference down in Edmonton and shut shit down up here once and for all.

BARRY: At least Greenpeace is there for Carmell and not sniffin' his savings away down at the bar.

TY grips the spade. LAURA enters, pursued by CARMELL.

CARMELL: The reason you keep asking about me and Ty is because you're not so sure any more about Barry.

LAURA: Barry and I are fine.

CARMELL: I see you talking to him and him not listening. I see you see him not listening and how you still go on talking anyway.

LAURA: My husband is not addicted to cocaine.

CARMELL: Nope, that's mine. But yours barely batted an eye after the game tonight.

LAURA stops.

I said, "Barry, we have an emergency," and he just stared at me. So then I had to get Ty—and he jumped into action like he'd just been waiting for me to give him some mission—

LAURA: I didn't mean for this to happen—I didn't mean for this to happen—I didn't mean for any of this to happen . . .

CARMELL: Well. What the fuck happened?!

Beat. TY smashes a Beetle with the flat end of the spade. LAURA bolts.

You have gotta be kidding me.

CARMELL runs after LAURA.

BARRY: That's right, let it all out. You're not to blame for your actions . . .

BARRY picks up the smashed Beetle like a little fallen soldier.

. . . the Longhorned Whitespotted Beetle is.

TY searches again.

TY: I am fuckin' sick and tired of feeling fuckin' bad about everything—like I should wake up every morning and apologize for being alive.

BARRY: Never apologize for being yourself, Ty—

TY: I won't apologize for my fuckin' truck nuts—

He brings the spade down.

BARRY: Nothing screams warrior like truck nuts and a court-mandated Breathalyzer—

TY: I won't apologize for telling Taryn's camp counsellors to go fuck themselves—

He brings the spade down.

I won't apologize for idling—

He brings the spade down.

I won't apologize for working in the oil industry—

He brings the spade down.

I won't apologize for setting Greenpeace's hybrid on fire—

He brings the spade down.

I won't apologize for setting this Forest on fire—

He brings the spade down.

I won't apologize for setting Fort McMurray on fire—

He brings the spade down weakly.

I was just bombin' around—bombin' around on my quad and sparks flew—

TY swings the spade wildly, like he's defending himself.

How was I supposed to know—how was I supposed to know it would grow into the inferno of the century?!

TY advances on BARRY.

So you wanna know who's been killin' all your birds and animals, Barry? Me. You wanna know who single-handedly raised the temperature on the planet a full degree? Me. You wanna know who brought Fort McMurray to its fuckin' knees? Me.

TY gets right in BARRY's face.

You wanna know who burned your house down, Barry? It was me.

TY and BARRY stare at each other. LAURA runs on and off.

You wanna hear takin' responsibility?

CARMELL chases after LAURA.

I killed six of your fuckin' Beetles, Barry.

BARRY: I should bury you here tonight.

TY: Do it.

BARRY lunges at TY.

BARRY: Do you think anyone would miss you, Ty? Do you think anyone would care if I buried you tonight?

TY: Fuckin' do it! I'm the guy who burned down your house, Barry.

They grapple.

You tell Haley it was her uncle Ty who burned down her house.

They grapple.

Bury me. Fuckin' bury me.

BARRY pushes TY into the grave, grabs the spade, and starts burying TY.

Bury me!

BARRY shovels.

Bury me!

BARRY shovels.

Bury me!

BARRY shovels.

Bury me!

LAURA runs through the Muskeg, entering and exiting.

I deserve to be buried.

CARMELL chases after LAURA, entering and exiting.

I deserve to be buried.

BARRY shovels.

I deserve to be buried . . .

BARRY shovels.

I deserve to die.

BARRY shovels.

I deserve to die . . .

BARRY finishes burying TY. He falls to the ground, gasping. LAURA enters, out of steam. CARMELL catches up, tackling her. The two struggle.

LAURA: You shouldn't have been listening to Barry's and my lovemaking!

CARMELL: I tried not to, desperately!

LAURA: That was an invasion of privacy!

CARMELL: You are living in my place!

LAURA: Do you think I want to be?!

CARMELL: You're not a guest—you're an occupying force!

LAURA: You don't even have CO2 detectors!

CARMELL: A lot of good they did you!

LAURA: It's your house that should've burned! You should be our guests! I've done everything right—everything right!

CARMELL: Except for tonight.

LAURA rolls into the fetal position. She moans, deep. TY erupts from the grave.

TY: My children will not be raised by Greenpeace!

TY grabs the spade and tries to press it against BARRY's throat.

How dare you tell Carmell to kick me out—

BARRY: That was her decision—

TY: Try to take my kids away from me—

BARRY: You can't even take care of yourself, Ty—

TY: You'd rather they be raised by the enemy!?

BARRY: Greenpeace isn't the enemy—

BARRY knocks the spade away.

The enemy is your wilful stupidity!

The two grapple on the ground.

CARMELL: I found you. After the game. Out back. Behind the Zamboni.

TY briefly pins BARRY.

TY: How would you like me to spend my time intelligently—to start dancing with Whooping Cranes!?

LAURA moans.

CARMELL: I took Wet Wipes. I washed your hands. Your face.

BARRY briefly pins TY.

BARRY: Maybe some time with the Whooping Cranes will remind you who you are!

BARRY and TY roll.

LAURA: We shouldn't have lost that game, Carmell.

LAURA swings her purse, bringing it down hard.

TY: You want me to start talking to the animals and the trees!?

BARRY: You might learn something!

TY: You want me to smoke a peace pipe with Greenpeace!?

BARRY: You shouldn't be smoking, or drinking, or sniffing anything!

BARRY and TY roll.

LAURA: For them to battle back like that . . . For them to battle back like that and for Taryn to win it.

BARRY: I'll gouge your fuckin' eyes out—

LAURA: Haley throwing off her glove and blocker . . .

TY: You don't have the balls—

LAURA: For them to battle back like that and to win it, to celebrate winning it, only to have the goal called back . . .

BARRY: You don't use 'em—

LAURA: Haley puts her glove and blocker back on . . .

BARRY: You don't need 'em—

LAURA: They drop the puck . . .

TY: But you and Greenpeace see everything—

LAURA: They go end to end—

TY: You see everything—

LAURA: They go top shelf on Haley . . .

The sound of a fire quickly grows.

And now the other team is celebrating . . .

The fire rages.

We shouldn't have lost that game!

LAURA *brings the purse down hard—a cosmic rupture.*

Silence.

I remember the fire
I remember the roar
I remember the fear
That we tried not to show

I remember the flames
I remember the madness
I remember the ash
As it fell like snowflakes
In silence

Pause.

Haley wrote that.

Pause.

The school counsellor had the kids write their feelings out. So they wouldn't keep them bottled up.

Pause.

I don't remember it like that. All I remember is the sound of blood rushing through my head. And the swish-swish of the wipers, in intervals, clearing ash from the windshield as we drove.

Pause.

To be a part of an exodus like that . . . An entire city, emptying out.

Pause.

The fire has shaken Haley's confidence in so many things.

Pause.

Except hockey.

Pause.

She still believes in hockey.

Pause.

When the evacuation order went out, the two things she grabbed were her mask and her pads.

Pause.

She's committed.

Pause.

Committed to her team. Committed to her community. Committed to being the best person she can be.

Long pause.

After we got let back into the city, I was making breakfast, at your place. Barry was at work and you were out with Declan doing something in the yard. Haley and Taryn were sitting at the kitchen table with Greenpeace, and Haley asked if he thought humans caused it. The fire. Greenpeace, he looked at Haley and Taryn and he said, "Yes. We caused it. And it won't be the last."

Haley and Taryn, they're waiting for their next batch of pancakes, staring into the pools of Saskatoon Berry syrup on their plates like they've just been given a sneak peek of the apocalypse . . . And I felt so powerless.

Pause.

So powerless to make them feel safe.

Pause.

And now Haley has these horrible dreams.

Long pause.

I have been so angry at you for introducing Greenpeace into our lives.

Silence.

BARRY: You fucking guy . . .

TY: I'm a liability, a major fuckin' liability . . .

BARRY *slowly stands, dusting himself off.*

What if it gets out? That I started it?

BARRY: It's not gonna get out.

TY: You can say that because you know how to keep your mouth shut . . . You're like a steel trap. I told anyone who would listen that I torched Greenpeace's hybrid—I can't keep my fuckin' mouth shut . . .

BARRY helps TY up.

There's gotta be a special place in hell for a guy who burns his own town down. If I'd'a not been out quading in the middle of the day when there was a fire advisory, sparkin' the inferno of the century, you'd still have your place . . . Haley would still have her Guinea Pigs . . . and we wouldn't be out here tonight . . .

Pause. BARRY starts digging again.

BARRY: Half of Fort McMurray thinks they started the fire, Ty. And the other half thinks it was Greenpeace.

BARRY digs in silence.

CARMELL: I don't dream.

Silence.

LAURA: How do you mean?

They breathe.

CARMELL: I sleep.

They breathe.

LAURA: Everybody has dreams.

They breathe. CARMELL shakes her head.

CARMELL: Then I don't remember anything.

They breathe.

So my nightmares are waking.

They breathe. They breathe.

Do you know what it was like? Covering for Ty on Christmas morning because he's been up all night partying, and Michael Bublé's Christmas special is playing on repeat?

They breathe. They breathe. They breathe.

Every time I hear Bublé on the radio now I'm reminded of how stupid I was not to kick Ty out long before I did. That I enabled him. That this fucking town enabled him.

They breathe. They breathe.

I can see the judgment in your eyes . . . in everybody's eyes . . . at Timmies . . . at the salon . . . at the rink . . . Like somebody who speaks openly about climate change is worse for me than a guy addicted to cocaine.

They breathe. They breathe. CARMELL *shakes her head.*

Fuck, I hate that guy.

They breathe.

LAURA: . . . Ty?

CARMELL: Bublé. When he starts scatting it's like somebody taking a drill to my brain.

They breathe. They breathe. BARRY *digs.* TY *begins to absently collect Sunflower shells.*

LAURA: We shouldn't have lost that game.

CARMELL: I know.

They breathe.

LAURA: We shouldn't be out here.

CARMELL: I know.

They breathe.

LAURA: I am so tired.

CARMELL: I know.

They breathe. They breathe.

LAURA: Do you think Ty and Barry . . .

CARMELL: They're fine.

LAURA: I would never forgive myself if I got them in trouble.

CARMELL: No one's getting in trouble—we just have to keep our cool.

They breathe. They breathe.

LAURA: Do you think I'm going to hell?

CARMELL: No.

LAURA: Mom would say I'm going to hell.

CARMELL: Mom thinks everyone's going to hell.

They breathe.

LAURA: After everything . . . after everything . . . I'm the weak link.

CARMELL: You're not.

LAURA: Why don't you turn me in? You need to protect yourself.

CARMELL: Because I don't know what I'd do without you, Laura.

They breathe.

You're like my lighthouse in a storm . . . annoying as hell, but I need you.

They breathe. They breathe.

LAURA: How?

They breathe.

CARMELL: At the rink that morning, when I suddenly started crying.

LAURA: You got ice melt in your eyes.

CARMELL *shakes her head.*

CARMELL: You believe everything I say . . .

LAURA: Why wouldn't I?

They breathe.

CARMELL: I was crying because I'd told Ty to leave. So you took over running the drills for me. And you were amazing.

LAURA: I was just copying what I'd seen you do a hundred times.

CARMELL: I never taught the girls to collapse to the net like that.

LAURA: You did.

CARMELL shakes her head.

CARMELL: You told the girls to circle the net like Muskox, to protect Haley from danger.

I definitely never said that.

CARMELL slowly stands, dusting herself off.

That's what I left the rink thinking that morning. That you and Barry and Mom and Dad were Muskox, circling me and Declan and Taryn, protecting us from what might come.

CARMELL helps LAURA up.

LAURA: I had no idea we were in a defensive formation.

CARMELL: Because you would have killed Tyson.

Pause.

So that's what Barry and Ty and I are doing tonight. We're protecting you, Laura.

They exit.

TY: Okay.

BARRY wipes sweat from his face. CARMELL and LAURA exit.

So, even if I'm not to blame . . . For causing the fire of the century . . . I'm still the same guy you told Carmy to leave.

BARRY digs.

BARRY: People can change. Slowly.

BARRY digs.

If you'd told me before the fire I'd be collecting dead birds and small mammals from around the ponds, carrying a two-headed Chickadee in my jacket pocket, I'd've said you were nuts.

Beat.

TY: You've . . .

Pause.

You've got it?

BARRY stops digging. He carefully takes a zip-lock out of his left jacket pocket and pulls out the Split Chickadee. BARRY hands the Split Chickadee to TY.

BARRY: It would've been able to see everything when it soared through the sky . . . Forwards and backwards, side to side . . .

Canada Geese in the distance.

If you'd told me before the fire that by the summer I'd feel like a stranger around Haley and Laura . . .

A cosmic flicker.

I've got so many questions swirling around in my mind. My fear is that they are gonna start spilling out and spilling out, and I'm not gonna be able to stop. So I've been turned. Inward. In on myself. I've not been there for Laura. Through a really hard time.

Canada Geese overhead. BARRY *and* TY *look to the sky.* LAURA *and* CARMELL *stand at the edge of a tailings pond.*

CARMELL: I don't think I've ever seen a tailings pond up close before . . .

They stare.

LAURA: Largest earthen structure on the planet.

They stare.

CARMELL: A testament to Canadian achievement.

They stare. They stare.

What do you think that says? That I asked Ty for help tonight but wouldn't dream of telling Greenpeace.

They stare. LAURA *shakes her head. They stare.*

People sweat different when they've lost their confidence.

They stare.

I . . . I miss the way Ty smelled before he started hating himself.

They stare. They stare. LAURA *shakes her head.*

LAURA: Barry hasn't said.

Pause.

Things aren't as rosy between me and Barry as I've been saying. He's been . . .

Pause.

In another place.

Pause.

He's been taking night classes. He's not gonna change careers or anything . . . The classes just provide . . .

CARMELL: A platform for learning.

LAURA: That's right.

TY produces the bag of Spitz. He offers them to BARRY without looking. BARRY accepts. They both pop seeds.

He's been studying Cree, taxidermy, entomology . . . That sort of thing.

TY spits.

When we evacuated and were staying at Barry's folks' place . . . that's when Barry started acting differently. We'd visited before, briefly, but Barry always avoided meeting his family in the community. I thought maybe because of the poverty, or because he was ashamed of me . . .

He'd go on these long walks, by himself and with his Elder . . . He went to a sweat with her . . . And when he came back, it was like he'd seen himself. Like, actually seen himself. And he didn't like what he saw.

When we got let back into the city, Barry started bringing home dead birds and small animals he'd find on his rounds around the ponds. He'd carry them like little fallen soldiers, like they were the most precious things in the world.

Long pause.

He found a two-headed Chickadee.

Pause.

CARMELL: How do you mean?

LAURA: Like a Chickadee. With two heads. And one body.

Pause.

He doesn't keep it in the deep freeze, like the rest of them. He thinks it's a sign, or something. So he drained it and stuffed it and keeps it in a zip-lock in his jacket pocket.

Pause.

CARMELL: Why?

Pause.

LAURA: To keep it close to his heart, I think.

Pause. TY *takes over digging.*

BARRY: What does that mean?

Pause.

When an entire city loses its ability to see?

Pause.

When the flames are literally at peoples' doorsteps, before the evacuation order goes out?

Long pause.

When we were stayin' with my folks, in Maskwacîs, my Elder told me about a prophecy, a Cree prophecy, that was made in 1949.

The prophecy said that the north would burn.

And work started up here right after.

Long pause.

Haley . . . She's been having trouble sleeping. All she sees when she closes her eyes are walls of flame.

Pause.

But those flames she's seeing . . . she told me, they're not from the fire that destroyed our home . . . They're from the fires to come.

Pause.

Are we as connected to this Forest as much as the Longhorned Whitespotted Beetle is, but we just don't wanna admit it?

Pause.

We've been here, on this land, for generations and generations. Has the work we've been doing led to the prophecy happening?

Pause.

What does this mean for Haley and Taryn and Declan? And for their children? And for their children's children?

Pause.

Haley and Taryn are excellent hockey players. But what have we taught them about their own cultures?

Pause.

How can we find balance in this place, between providing for our families but not ignoring our other responsibilities?

Pause.

And can that balance even be achieved . . . ? Or is it too late?

TY digs in silence.

TY: I'm not someone who should be giving advice . . .

TY digs.

But I think it's okay to have these questions on your mind.

TY digs.

Carrying around a two-headed Chickadee is . . . strange. But if there's anybody who might understand the questions you're having, it's Laura and Carmy and me, Barry.

TY digs.

We are under an immense amount of pressure . . . "An immense amount of sociological pressure," says that therapist that I'm going to. He tells me this is a time to reflect. To take stock of my life. To be the change I want to see. Or be. Or be, then see. Like I've been doin' somethin' wrong up to this point. Like I suddenly don't belong in my own life.

TY stops digging and stares at the moon.

But when we were escaping the fire . . . Havin' Carm 'n' Declan 'n' Taryn riding with me again . . .

Pause.

And then we got to Edmonton . . . and I was alone. Just wandering around West Edmonton Mall. Rented one of those private cabanas at the water park, like we had in Vallarta, but it was just me . . . surrounded by all these families.

And all I'm thinkin' is how all I want is to be back in my truck, drivin' down the highway with my family again.

Pause. TY starts digging again.

You said it's like I'm happy bein' out here. Digging. And you're right. 'Cause for the first time, in a long time, Carm needs me for something. And that is the best feeling.

TY digs.

I am addicted to cocaine. And Spitz, I think. I am not going to be able to snap my fingers and magically unfuck my life. But maybe, if I'm gentle and honest with myself and others, I can alter my destructive patterns and slowly unfuck my life.

TY digs in silence.

BARRY: That should do 'er, Tyson.

TY stops digging. They stare at the open grave.

Let's get 'er done.

TY nods. They exit.

CARMELL: After the game, I found you. Standing. Behind the Zamboni.

LAURA: After we lost . . . I left the bench. I walked down the hallway. I went to the parking lot, out back, behind the Zamboni . . .

Pause.

And then he came out . . .

Pause.

He walked right past . . .

I said, "Where are you going? The game can't end this way."

And he just kept walking past.

Pause.

So I . . .

Pause.

I . . .

Pause.

I . . .

Pause.

I ripped the truck nuts off of Ty's truck . . . And bashed him over the head.

TY and BARRY enter carrying a hockey bag between them. They set the bag down, unzip it, and tumble out a dead ref.

TY: Cold as ice.

BARRY: Yup.

TY prods the ref with his foot.

TY: And stiff.

BARRY: That's how we'll all get.

Pause. BARRY and TY awkwardly struggle to get the ref straight in the pit. They get the ref to fit. A sonic cannon fires.

LAURA: Sonic cannons. To discourage birds from landing on the ponds.

Sounds of Snow Geese flying overhead.

Snow Geese. Snow Geese, I think.

LAURA smiles, staring at the Snow Geese. TY and BARRY fill the grave.

I'm a killer.

Pause.

CARMELL: Just because you killed someone doesn't mean you're a killer.

Pause.

LAURA: It's pretty neat how our daughters are so close. Cousins. But best friends.

CARMELL nods. Silence.

What do you think our child selves would say if they saw us here, Carmell?

CARMELL: I dunno.

Pause.

I think they'd be proud.

LAURA: Huh.

CARMELL: That no matter what . . . we stuck together. We stood our ground.

Pause. LAURA smiles and nods. Pause.

What do you think that says? That I asked Ty for help with this but wouldn't dream of telling Greenpeace.

Pause. LAURA shakes her head. Pause. TY and BARRY have finished filling the grave. They stare at it.

LAURA: It's nice being out here with you.

CARMELL: Mm.

LAURA: Just a couple of sisters, stargazing in Alberta.

They smile. LAURA slowly opens her purse. She pulls out bloody, galvanized truck nuts. TY nods. BARRY nods. They exit, TY carrying the spade.

CARMELL nods at LAURA. LAURA goes to throw the truck nuts into the tailings pond. Cross-fade. BARRY and TY sit at BPS, BARRY with a beer, TY with a pitcher of Diet Pepsi. LAURA and CARMELL enter with fishbowls.

CARMELL: Hey.

BARRY: Hey.

TY: Hey.

LAURA: Hey.

Silence.

TY: Bugs were pretty bad, eh?

The three stare at TY. *Silence.*

LAURA: I just wanna say . . .

Long pause.

I just wanna say . . .

Pause.

That I am grateful.

Pause.

I am so grateful to be with you all here tonight.

The four stare at each other.

Fishbowl Friday.

They hold up their drinks.

End of play.

THE PARTICULARS

FOREWORD

BY SIMON BRACKEN

The late dramaturge Iris Turcott, mentor to Matthew MacKenzie and a champion of many Canadian theatre artists, described (with admiration and I suspect some ambivalence) *The Particulars* as something one might find in *The New Yorker*. I have always imagined the play works in part because Matthew was honest enough to recount something deeply personal, which, as the writing adage goes, became universal. But the literary quality has been for me its key.

What wins the audience to Gordon almost immediately, what makes him endearing and, at times, bizarrely adorable, is his third-person address. Gordon is talking of himself and addressing us, ostensibly. There should be no fourth wall, and yet there is, created through his improbable, rigid grammar. As Gordon removes himself from reality and from us, he writes of his experience as opposed to relaying it. The audience therefore watches in real time, but listens to Gordon with all the affect of reading him. His attention to detail, his barrage of bold opinions and stark assessments, his alien and paradoxically rapacious need to remain calm and ordered and good make for a hilarious journey through an unerringly mundane suburban life.

Reading, however, is a solitary venture—in so far as it requires our own voice, that is its message. Gordon is using this innate, human, automatic intimacy to signal there is more, to tell us what he adamantly can't. Where the fuelled text should be a straightforward appeal, by choosing to write it for our own discovery we hear much more: private disclosure, a laden confession. Where he chooses obvious—and admitted—bombast, we find furtive terror. From the beginning, Gordon is up there against the fates, against himself, and yet somehow, because each reader is forced to come to Gordon on their own, this is almost a clandestine affair.

Gordon is doing what good writers do: he is creating a dialogue beneath the words, the uncovered intimacy of which adds charge to those spoken and compels us to turn the page. Gordon, of course, turns it for you, and just when you realize the depths from which this is written, slams the book shut.

I love playing Gordon. I'm suited for him, somehow, and the audience, in the way that I've described, always wants more and more of you, and that is exhilarating in a way few things are; it's the closest I'll come to flying. But what I really love is the dawning realization of them, out there beyond the light, usually around the hockey segment (though I couldn't for the life of me tell you why). They surface long enough to marvel that this is a play.

Simon Bracken is a Canadian actor. Aside from playing Gordon on many occasions, his work includes performances with the Royal Manitoba Theatre Centre, Shakespeare in the Ruff, Coal Mine Theatre, and the Stratford Festival. He trained at the National Theatre School of Canada, and lives in Toronto.

A first iteration of *The Particulars* was produced at the Montreal Fringe in 2008, directed by Patrick Lundeen, designed by Chiharu Ono, and featuring Alex Furber as Gordon.

The play was later produced by Punctuate! Theatre at The Theatre Centre, Toronto, from October 17 to 26, 2019, followed by a production at La Cité Francophone, Edmonton, from November 1 to 2, 2019. It featured the following cast and creative team:

Gordon: Simon Bracken

Writer and Director: Matthew MacKenzie
Choreographer: Alida Kendell
Producer: Sheiny Satanove
Stage Manager: Kai-Yueh Chen
Rehearsal Stage Manager: Beth Dart
Lighting Designer: Kaileigh Krysztofiak
Production Manager: Trent J. Crosby
Chorus Dancers: Amber Borotsik, Lara Ebata, Bridget Jessome, Richard Lee, Krista Lin, Rebecca Sadowski, Kate Stashko, and Raena Waddell

CHARACTERS

Gordon

This play can be performed solo, or with a Chorus of dancers

A summer storm—we catch fleeting glimpses of GORDON *in a housecoat and the* CHORUS *in veils in a dramatic movement sequence. The storm passes and* GORDON *and the* CHORUS *spin out in ecstatic anguish. We hear them breathing in the darkness.*

Lights slowly rise on GORDON *and the* CHORUS, *the housecoat and the veils discarded. Silence.*

GORDON: The scratching began soon after the renovations had been completed. A toxic fog still hung in the air throughout the house, the painters having used a satin enamel finish on all baseboards and subsequent trim. Going against his better judgment, Gordon had agreed to the application, taking the contractor's word that the fumes would dissipate soon after project completion.

Like many people, Gordon could not sleep with noise: the dripping of a tap, the breathing of a loved one, neighbours from Newfoundland. And, ever since he had been sleeping alone, Gordon had found it impossible to ignore odour. He was unable to block scent.

The job had been finished for over a week, but still the fumes had not died . . . So Gordon would lie awake, organizing the next day's tasks in his head, lest the nightly episode prove a total exercise in frustration.

GORDON *faces front.*

On the particular night the scratching began, a storm had been passing outside.

The CHORUS *travel.*

Wind whipped wood chips and topsoil around the yard, while the rain badly damaged the Delphiniums . . .

The CHORUS *come to a crooked stillness.*

The front passed as quickly as it had come . . . but something remained. Scratching.

Something alive. Something very busy.

GORDON *listens.*

Gordon's newly installed sound-suppression drywall—which evidently kept noise in as well as it kept noise out—told Gordon that the scratching came from within. No question.

GORDON *listens.*

Trying to isolate the area from which the activity originated proved impossible though, as the home's calculated acoustics made for a kind of surround-sound irritant. But no.

No.

The scratching had stopped outright.

Gordon lay motionless, his breathing shallow. Nothing.

The only sound was that of the south-face downspout, which, due to blockage or improper assembly, was emptying at a much slower rate than the rest.

The CHORUS *sink.*

Sunday.

The CHORUS *correct.*

Gordon began the week at church, catching the nine a.m. early service.

Gordon always sat in the balcony, as the pew cushions on the main level had been stuffed with Horse hair, to which Gordon had a severe allergy that made it difficult to breathe—like someone was kneeling on his chest.

As attendance at the early service was generally half that of the noon, Gordon usually sat alone.

The CHORUS *in formation.*

To begin, the congregation was informed that Reverend Wishart would not be preaching . . . as he had sustained a lower-body injury at the annual clergy road-hockey game and had been left temporarily incapacitated.

Apparently, late in the match with the teams tied, Reverend Wishart had fallen on the ball during a mad scramble. Then, having concealed the ball between his legs, had stumbled in feigned agony towards the opposing team's net. By the time the Anglicans realized what was happening, Reverend Wishart had made it to within five feet of the goal, where he was cut down.

The CHORUS *hit the ground.*

But—

The CHORUS *correct, then hit the ground again in slow motion.*

—as he fell, Wishart managed to get a shot away, going topside on the bishop, before subsequently being rushed to emergency.

The CHORUS *carry Jesus on the cross.*

Reverend Wishart's stand-in was the youth minister, Reverend Lillian McKeown, who used a recent trip to the equatorial jungles of central Africa as the subject of her sermon. During this oration . . . Gordon got to thinking that Squirrels could probably not swim.

The CHORUS *travel.*

In an attempt to escape the storm—the downpour of the night before—one had likely taken refuge in the chimney. While dry, the darkness, combined with the soot, would have worked to create a great deal of confusion, which would explain the desperate scratching that followed the rain.

The CHORUS *in stillness.*

The thought of the Squirrel returning to his family was a chilling one.

The CHORUS *morph.*

Half-drowned, and then caked in filth from the chute, the Squirrel's appearance would have been completely altered—the other Squirrels mistaking him for an intruder and attacking.

The CHORUS *are cut down.*

It had been Gordon's experience that some of the cutest things in life were often the fiercest. Like feral Cats, little big men, and Chickadees.

The CHORUS *correct.*

Concluding her sermon . . . Reverend McKeown shared how the Forest people of equatorial Africa's central Jungles believe that when they sing, the echo from the trees is the Forest answering. That if bad things are happening, it is because the Forest is sleeping. And that when someone dies . . . their soul leaves their body as a tiny winged being.

Fairy shimmer.

After church, Gordon returned home to deal with the yard.

The CHORUS *become crooked.*

Of the thirty-seven Delphiniums, six had snapped and needed to be disposed of, while thirteen required immediate support with twist-ties and bamboo . . .

The CHORUS *twitch.*

During this operation, Gordon discovered Aphids in the north-east-face flower bed, gorging themselves on the sap of the blue and purple Delphiniums.

GORDON *corrects.*

Using his synthetic feather duster, Gordon gently brushed the soft-headed opportunists off the exposed stems.

The CHORUS *stop twitching.*

Upon closer inspection, Gordon learned that the south-face down-spout was blocked from above. Debris had collected where the spout met the eaves, meaning that water had overflowed, pooling above the south-face foundation. As a result, the Old Gold Juniper was almost completely submerged.

The CHORUS *travel—a cyclone.*

In an effort to save the shrub and his basement from potential flood damage, Gordon drained the area with his wet/dry shop-vac.

The CHORUS *in storm retrograde.*

Next, Gordon replenished the depleted topsoil, raked the wood chips back to their original positions, then boarded the chimney.

Everything in order, Gordon retired to the kitchen to prepare his contribution for the evening's buffet.

Sunday was movie night, when interested adults in the congregation would return to the church basement to watch a weekly old-time feature. Each member of the Cinema Club was required to bring a small snack or refreshment for the group, and, for a bit of a splash, this week Gordon was bringing baba ganouj.

A flourish.

As most members of the Cinema Club were either widows or widowers who liked to get to bed early, the screening always began at six o'clock sharp—no exceptions.

Mrs. Wisniewski had brought in *Camille*, which she introduced as a love story "borrowed from the French."

Mrs. Wisniewski, who had promised her dying husband that she would never remarry, had the habit of repeating out loud her favourite lines as they were delivered by her favourite heroines—a habit she was unaware she had.

The CHORUS *in shadow,* GORDON *in movie light.*

For *Camille*, she sat quiet throughout, until, nearing the end, with death threatening, Greta Garbo and Mrs. Wisniewski whispered, "Let me love you. Let me live for you. I ask nothing more from Heaven than that."

The CHORUS *reach for* GORDON *through the shadows.*

With his baba ganouj a hit, Gordon returned home and decided to call it an early night, Sunday being the day of rest.

The CHORUS *correct.*

Before bed, Gordon fed the Cats, sprayed the Vanda Teres Gigantea Orchid, prayed, and turned off the lights.

GORDON *listens. The* CHORUS *shake.*

The moment Gordon lay down, the scratching began, again.

Holding his breath, Gordon silently pulled back his sheets and slipped into his slippers, noting that they would pad his approach. Keeping to the walls so that the shadows would not betray him, Gordon tiptoed through his home.

The kitchen.

No question.

Lights—the CHORUS *in stillness.*

The second Gordon hit the lights, though, the scratching stopped. Outright.

Lights shift.

Monday, the normal routine.

The CHORUS *corrects.* GORDON *begins to dress—an undershirt, dress socks.*

Gordon was well-liked by his co-workers. People dug his ties and how he bit his words without sounding aggressive.

As most communication at the office was done over email, Gordon always paid close attention to his net-i-quette. He would always read each message he sent three times to ensure proper tone, being careful to come across respectful and approachable, while trying to avoid sounding curt or demanding. He never wrote in all upper case, as this read like shouting, and he never wrote in all lower case, as this read like mumbling. Contractions were all right, as they conveyed an easy, conversational tone, but slang, under any circumstance, was not okay.

After work, Gordon stopped off at Planet Organic to pick up what he would need for dinner. Four years previous, Gordon had taken a nine-day vacation to Cancún. While he had rarely left his room, the cuisine had left an impression.

His purchases included Avocado, refried Beans, Cactus strips, organic Lemon juice, Garlic, Pineapple, Red Pepper, Sesame Seeds, free-trade Corn tortilla chips, tofu, and all the fixin's. Monday was taco night. The Pineapple he would use at a later date.

Gordon's mother had been a busy woman. Busy in the head. She was unable to function unless all things to do with her were in constant flux. Gordon had taken it quietly, in the stomach, lest she focus all her energies on him. By his fifteenth birthday, the ulcers were so severe that Gordon's diet had to be altered, and a vegan of necessity was born.

The CHORUS *on their knees, palms to the sky.*

Back at home, Gordon went out to the garden to pick Cilantro, Romaine Lettuce, and Cherry Tomatoes.

The CHORUS *begin to twitch.*

Rather than moving on to greener pastures, the Aphids had returned.

GORDON *observes.*

The tiny pear-shaped pests, for this round, had apparently enlisted protectors.

GORDON dusts.

Every time Gordon went to brush Aphids from a Delphinium, Ants would swarm, attacking his duster with such ferociousness that Gordon was forced to step back and reassess his approach.

GORDON takes a knee. A member of the CHORUS slowly begins to undulate.

When left undisturbed, it could be observed that the Ants were in fact not only defending but tending the Aphids—tickling their tummies with their antennae, and then harvesting the shiny goo the Aphids had been gently compelled to excrete.

Having heard of the phenomenon of Aphid farming and now actually witnessing Aphids being actively milked produced two very different reactions in Gordon, as he stood trying to disguise his disgust with the sometimes graphic nature of an otherwise affectionate mutualistic relationship.

GORDON stands.

Crushing six cloves of Garlic to create a potent plant-based repellent, Gordon sprayed the northeast-face flower bed in an effort to discourage the Aphids and their handlers from doing any more damage.

The CHORUS stop twitching and undulating.

Following dinner, Gordon searched the kitchen for holes and/or other points of entry. He moved the oven and the fridge, discovering nothing behind them, except that the area needed a good scrub. Next were the cupboards, which he emptied then reordered, bagging and sealing any would-be food sources.

Before bed, Gordon fed the Cats, sprayed the Vanda Teres Gigantea Orchid, prayed, and turned off the lights.

GORDON listens. The CHORUS vibrate.

Scratching.

As before.

Clear and workmanlike.

GORDON listens. The CHORUS's vibrations grow.

Gordon lay for fifty-four minutes, hoping that once the intruder determined there was no easy meal to be had, they would be on their way.

The CHORUS gyrate.

The scratching, though, did not subside, but rather steadily increased in intensity, until Gordon was forced to investigate.

GORDON travels.

Entering in darkness, Gordon surveyed the kitchen, his eyes having grown accustomed to the moonlight.

The CHORUS are still.

No movement.

The scratching had ceased, abruptly.

The only sign of any activity was the Pineapple, which showed signs of having been nibbled.

The CHORUS slowly correct.

Tuesday saw Gordon go about his normal routine, the previous night's scratching not impacting on his workday performance. The Pineapple had been purchased for consumption, not for bait, but as such it would clearly function just fine.

On his way home from work, Gordon stopped at the all-purpose store and picked up four catch-and-release traps.

The CHORUS *stand with their backs to* GORDON.

Todd, the cashier, informed his co-cashier that catch-and-release traps were for chicks and fags—like coupons and compromise. Having lived a vegan for over a decade in harmony with the animal kingdom, no Greek retailer pretending to be Italian was going to upset Gordon's balance now.

GORDON *puts on his shoes.*

Following a little Chickpea curry and pickled-Beat salad, Gordon made sure to turn on the game. Sports had never exactly appealed to Gordon, but office dynamics made the almost bi-nightly chore necessary.

In his first week with the company, Gordon had learned that a male employee's fate lay largely in his ability to talk hockey. The unspoken rules associated with this practice were many.

Realizing he could not compensate for a lifetime of disinterest, Gordon had developed a system. In an effort to discourage anyone from asking questions, Gordon would often let drop a devastatingly specific statistic, like, "We've scored more third-period goals against teams from the west coast than anyone else in the league." Or, "Pittsburgh has been called on more stick infractions than the next three teams combined." These stats afforded Gordon a certain quiet confidence.

In the event of a loss, when knowledge of the game came under even closer scrutiny, Gordon targeted a certain Finnish player. Although one of the more skilled individuals on the team, this player had a name which was difficult to pronounce. Gordon decided to hate this player, and in the event of a loss, would cite his favourite whipping boy, taking special pleasure in pronouncing his name improperly. The strategy even worked when the player wasn't in the lineup.

Tactics aside though, the most important feature to the conversations was attitude. Gordon, like the rest, operated with a lot of bombast, but not a lot of content.

Content threatens people and "Gordo" did not wish to be perceived a threat.

GORDON's shoes are on.

After the game, Gordon went to inspect the northeast-face flower bed.

The CHORUS contort.

The Aphids had spread.

The CHORUS link in vine canon.

Following the Honeysuckle vine as the route the insects had obviously taken, Gordon discovered that the northeast- and northwest-face flower beds now bore parasitic colonies, each tended by a battle group of Ants.

The CHORUS in reverse military canon.

Trimming the Honeysuckle vine back, Gordon sprayed both flower beds with a double dose of his homemade repellent, this time adding a little Cayenne to the mix.

The CHORUS writhe. GORDON prepares the Pineapple.

Before bed, Gordon generously baited the traps with the spoilt Pineapple, fed the Cats, sprayed the Vanda Teres Gigantea Orchid, prayed, and turned off the lights.

Cross-fade—a lunar eclipse. The CHORUS *violently vibrate, contained.*

That night, Gordon lay, listening to the scratching, which became more frantic as the night wore on. Gordon imagined that he too would work himself into a panic if, after eating his weight in Ananas, found himself confined to a box.

Cross-fade—the end of a solar eclipse.

On Wednesdays, Gordon woke before dawn. Rain or shine, he always met the middle of the week with a walk through the Valley. First dawn being a primary feeding time, Gordon exited through the front door rather than the back, not wishing to disturb anyone breakfasting in the kitchen.

Gordon's route took him down along the water, the path then cutting through a park, which was popular with sweethearts and the ultimate Frisbee crowd. The park presently sat nameless, the long-deceased former title holder having been recently identified by the NDP as a proponent of a state-sponsored eugenics program during the dirty thirties.

A battered band of Chickadees had taken refuge in the park two years previous, a move which directly coincided with the city's elimination of the bird pest-control position.

Concerned largely with the reduction of Crow and Magpie numbers to ensure the survival of indigenous songbird populations, the bird pest-control agent had been recorded by a film crew from Germany taking Magpie hatchlings from their nest and drowning them in a bucket. When aired, the footage created such a furor in Europe that the city was forced to capitulate and eliminate the bird pest-control position in the face of an aggressive letter-writing campaign.

While obviously wanting to see the Magpies relocated rather than drowned, Gordon questioned the wisdom of taking instruction from a continent whose wildlife consisted almost entirely of Rats, Pigeons, and neo-Nazis.

With nothing to stop them, Crows and Magpies had multiplied in excess, quickly asserting total dominance in the region, carrying out innumerable massacres of their own against their musically inclined brethren.

The band of Chickadees had survived the purge, but the difficult times had left them paranoid and edgy.

Each week, as Gordon walked through the area where the Poplars met the brush, a sentry would sound the alarm and the Chickadees would go ballistic. Darting back and forth across the path in a flurry of wings and "dee-dees," the band would create a calculated commotion, in what Gordon reasoned was an attempt to exaggerate their numbers.

Emerging from the brush, Gordon would take the stairs, briefly entering the downtown core to make his weekly floral purchase. Every Wednesday, without fail, Gordon purchased fresh-cut flowers. These arrangements were generally put together by the proprietor, so long as she followed two rules. First, the flowers needed to be fresh, not open, so that they would later bloom.

The CHORUS *bloom, then close.*

Second, no Gerberas, Roses, or Lilies. Gordon had determined that Gerberas, Roses, and Lilies are to the flower kingdom what Pigeons, Crows, and Magpies were to the bird—so common they had become offensive.

With his bouquet in hand, Gordon returned home, where he immediately went into the kitchen to inspect the traps. Save for the Pineapple rinds, which evidently had held no appeal, the traps were empty.

Consequently, during work hours, Gordon was forced to research alternative pest-control options.

Inaudible to humans, the Pest Repeller created the strongest ultrasonic, high-pitched, siren-like sound on the market. Gordon purchased three pest-repelling devices from the all-purpose store and triangulated their positions in his kitchen, thereby maximizing their intended effect.

Following a quick Seaweed smoothie, Gordon found that the Aphids had continued their march, the sapsuckers and their rabid defenders spreading to the southeast-face flower bed.

Getting in to his hybrid, Gordon drove twenty-three kilometres outside of the city to a pesticide-free greenhouse nursery, where he purchased a Ladybug colony—the Aphids' natural enemy.

Releasing the spotted ladies in the compromised flower beds, Gordon then took care of the backlog of paperwork from the day.

Gordon always completed his assigned tasks on time, quality above standard, enjoying special standing in the eyes of middle management, all of whom were women. A disastrous flirt, Gordon was known as a gentleman for all occasions, the status he enjoyed not sexually derived, but rather born out of consistency, respect, and his signature "yes ma'am" approach.

After completing the day's work, Gordon powered up his *Dance Dance Revolution* game console.

Ever since college, Gordon had hit the club on hump day—cheap drinks, mad beats, and every so often a special someone met a special somebody else. While it had been some time since Gordon had been out, he continued the wild Wednesdays tradition religiously.

GORDON *dances. The* CHORUS *are still.*

Before bed, Gordon fed the Cats, sprayed the Vanda Teres Gigantea Orchid, prayed, and turned off the lights.

Cross-fade.

Throughout the night, desperate scratching could be heard, the sonic sirens no doubt reaching monumentally irritating levels.

Long cross-fade.

Four years previous, Gordon's fiancé had been hit by a bus and instantly killed. While only a seedling at the time, their Vanda Teres Gigantea Orchid had since blossomed on numerous occasions, becoming a living representation of the love the two had shared.

Lights slowly rise.

Thursday found Gordon standing in his kitchen . . . a kitchen in disarray . . .

The CHORUS *stand, their palms to the sky.*

His most precious of possessions deflowered.

Fairy shiver.

Thursday.

The CHORUS *start to shake, then lurch, then thrash.*

While at his desk, Gordon mused that there was nothing more natural than the struggle between cat and mouse, an age-old struggle, pitting Feline speed and agility against the Rodent knack for burrowing and multiplying at a ridiculous rate.

The CHORUS *turns on itself.*

For several years, Gordon had been feeding two neighbourhood Cats.

The CHORUS *stamp in unison.*

The first was a stray who did not like to be touched, who Gordon had named Ché.

The CHORUS *stamp twice.*

Ché was an abnormally large Tiger Tabby who Gordon had saved.

A flurry of wings.

Going through the Valley one morning, Gordon had happened upon a Coyote . . . the two staring at each other in stillness as the sun rose.

During this silence, Gordon had watched Ché approach, stalking from behind, then clawing the Coyote in the hindquarters. As it quickly became apparent, Ché had not thought much beyond the initial instigation.

GORDON *advances, the* CHORUS *scatter.*

By the time Gordon had chased the Coyote off, Ché was unconscious, his jaw dislocated, his tail hanging by a thread.

GORDON *stands, palms to the sky.*

The emergency veterinary bill had been more than three thousand dollars, as Gordon had been required by law to pay for Ché's shots, get him neutered, and have him dewormed, in addition to the cost of the surgery performed on Ché's jaw and tail, the reattachment of which the veterinarian had deemed cosmetic.

Gordon had brought Ché home, but no sooner had Ché regained his health than the living situation became untenable.

GORDON *drops his hands.*

Gordon worried that the stray harboured some ill will towards him, for while it was true he had saved the Tiger Tabby from death's grip, he had subsequently been financially implicated in the removal of Ché's manhood.

Ché still came around for dinner, but would only eat under the auspices he was stealing from Mr. Humphrey.

Mr. Humphrey was the neighbours' Persian, who, if it was a child, would be classified a victim of neglect. An irregular diet consisting predominantly of beernuts and white Russians had left Mr. Humphrey docile.

The CHORUS *stagger walk.*

Each evening, Gordon would prepare one feeding station—one feeding station with enough food to feed three cats. The meal generally played out in the same way, although Ché constantly changed his hiding place from which he would ambush. First, Mr. Humphrey would come and inspect the dish. Then, out of nowhere, Ché would pounce, with Mr. Humphrey cowering and Gordon feigning surprise. Next, Ché would eat his fill, generally twice that of a normal cat. Mr. Humphrey, after patiently waiting, would then have his dinner, a meal rich in nutrients and vitamins essential for a long-haired cat.

All Gordon needed to do was let nature run its course; by enlisting the help of his Feline friends, his home would be rid of a stubborn nuisance and the Cats would have their customary five-star meal.

The CHORUS *stamp three times—military.*

The Ladybug colony had fared poorly.

The CHORUS *begin to gyrate, collapsing to the ground.*

Their own deterrent of playing dead and bleeding from the ankles to discourage attackers had triggered disaster, seemingly serving to only incense the Ants further.

The Ants, after swarming, would carry the Ladybugs away, on bloody display for the whole garden to see.

The CHORUS *are carried limply away.*

Only a few shell-shocked survivors remained, unable to take flight. Their wings had been clipped by the green horde's rabid defenders, each spotted lady running in crooked counter-clockwise circles, waiting their turn to be carried off like Chickens to the slaughter.

A newcomer could be observed in the midst of the bloated herd, a twitching larva with bright red markings and fuzzy antennae.

While the Ants harassed and tormented the Ladybugs, they allowed the larva to feed freely on the Aphids.

GORDON *and the* CHORUS *bring one hand up.*

Consulting his *Indigenous Plant and Insect Guide of Wildrose Country*, Gordon learned that the larva was that of the threatened Red Frosted Elfin Butterfly.

GORDON *and the* CHORUS *bring the other hand up.*

Accepting that the Aphids could now only be managed rather than eliminated, lest he risk further endangering Elfin numbers, Gordon took alternative measures.

Red Elfin flutter.

Cutting the bottoms off seventy-four biodegradable cups, Gordon slathered each in molasses, then placed them at the bottom of each infested plant.

Whirling dervish.

The cups in position, Gordon then took care of some correspondence.

Each week, images were emailed around by men at the office, of the pornographic variety. The female body did not bother Gordon, just the way it was presented.

The Internet disturbed Gordon, as he had found it nearly impossible to browse for his weekly submission without repeatedly stumbling on the most unspeakable images. Unfortunately, office dynamics dictated he remedy the situation. Gordon had decided he would be a lingerie man.

For Thursday's submission, Gordon selected an image titled "Killer Thong."

The strange appeal associated with women's underpants had always been lost on Gordon. How something tantamount to dental floss for the ass could excite the senses was beyond his understanding.

As Gordon's images were often a good deal tamer than the rest, he would sex things up by changing the image's title. For this, he would return to hockey.

Hockey move.

These titles, Gordon learned, did not need bear any relation to a specific player or game—they weren't even required to make sense. For "Killer Thong," Gordon substituted, "This One's Goin' to Video Review."

Rapid abstracted hockey motif replay.

He pressed send then began setting up the feeding station as he always did, only this time he took care to put the Cat food inside, rather than outside, the kitchen door. Gordon waited for Mr. Humphrey to inspect, Ché to ambush and then begin on his meal, before shutting the Cats in.

That night, as Gordon lay awake, he listened to the Cats in the kitchen, busy with their work.

Dance of the macabre.

Come morning, Gordon ventured into the kitchen to find it turned completely upside down . . .

Distant funeral march.

Lying under the breakfast nook, Ché slept soundly on top of the partially cannibalized remains of Mr. Humphrey.

The CHORUS *stamp slowly, three times.*

Judging by the state of the room, the stray had made some sport of the domestic.

An abstracted replay.

Lest the neighbours be alerted to their loss, Gordon wrapped Mr. Humphrey in plastic sheeting, then placed him in a duffle bag. Taking only a small garden spade so as to not attract attention, Gordon walked to the park, finding a secluded spot for the burial.

GORDON *is harassed.*

As he dug, a Chickadee sentry sounded the alarm. What began as a flurry quickly became a maelstrom, as the smell of cat and blood caught the morning air.

Desperately trying to sever roots and dig deeper, Gordon was forced repeatedly to cover his head and face as the Chickadees circled and dove in their madness.

GORDON *is tormented.*

Arriving at the office a half-hour late, Friday saw Gordon greeted by a rep from middle management, who was waiting for him in his cubicle when he arrived at work. In his haste to prepare the feeding stations the night before, Gordon had inadvertently sent his weekly porn submission to the entire company email list and all its subsidiaries.

"O Fortuna."

After collecting and boxing his things, Gordon returned home . . .

GORDON is carried away like the spotted ladies, on bloody display for the whole office to see.

. . . where he discovered that the Aphids had spread to the vegetable garden . . .

The CHORUS writhe beneath GORDON.

. . . the Red Frosted Elfin having formed a cocoon amongst the Aubergine.

The CHORUS shake and spasm, reaching for GORDON.

Though not even midday, sustained scratching could be heard from the kitchen throughout the house.

GORDON steps free from the CHORUS, but they are quickly all around him again.

Calmly rising, Gordon walked to the garage and drove to the all-purpose store. Without a word, he purchased the Snap-Trap 2000, which guaranteed a kill or your money back.

Upon returning home, Gordon took the stepladder from out of the shed and the flowers he had purchased—which were now in full bloom. Then, as he always did, Gordon walked the three and a half blocks to the marked crosswalk, climbed the ladder, and tied the flowers to the unmarked sign . . .

The CHORUS *bloom. Cross-fade.*

Saturday.

Gordon lay in bed until three thirty-seven p.m., when, from his bedroom, he observed the Red Frosted Elfin emerge from its cocoon and fly from his garden . . .

GORDON *watches the Red Frosted Elfin fly from his garden, then observes his yard, overrun with Aphids.* GORDON *slashes and burns his garden.*

Later that night, while lying in bed awake, Gordon noted that the fumes had finally died, nearly twelve days after the contractor had made his promise—nearly eight days longer than it had taken the contractor to complete the project . . .

Snap!

In an instant Gordon was out of bed—dashing through the house—bursting into the kitchen—dropping to his knees in front of the trap.

Little legs, little arms, a little face, little wings . . . a little orchid dress . . .

GORDON *slowly stands.*

It had been four years, one month, two weeks, and six days since magic had left Gordon's life. Killing the fairy served to confirm the fact.

A citizen of the Métis Nation of Alberta, Matthew MacKenzie is a multi-award-winning playwright from amiskwaciwâskahikan (Edmonton). Artistic Director of Punctuate! Theatre, Matthew is Founder and an Artistic Associate with Pyretic Productions, a founding member of the Pemmican Collective, as well as Canadian Liaison of the Liberian Dance Troupe. Matthew has had nearly a dozen of his works produced across Turtle Island.